Baking with Candy

Baking with CANDY

JENNY WARSÉN

Skyhorse Publishing

First published by Bonnier Fakta in 2016

First Skyhorse Publishing Edition 2018

Text copyright © 2016 by Jenny Warsén
Photography by Ulrika Pousette
Graphic design by Lisa Kullberg
Edited by Annika Ström
Repro Italgraf Media AB, Stockholm
Tryck Livonia Print, Lettland 2016

Skyhorse Publishing books may be purchased in bulk at special discounts for sales promotion, corporate gifts, fund-raising, or educational purposes. Special editions can also be created to specifications. For details, contact the Special Sales Department, Skyhorse Publishing, 307 West 36th Street, 11th Floor, New York, NY 10018 or info@skyhorsepublishing.com.

Skyhorse® and Skyhorse Publishing® are registered trademarks of Skyhorse Publishing, Inc.®, a Delaware corporation.

Visit our website at www.skyhorsepublishing.com.

10 9 8 7 6 5 4 3 2 1

Library of Congress Cataloging-in-Publication Data is available on file.

Cover design by Michael Short
Cover and interior photography by Ulrika Pousette

ISBN: 978-1-5107-3018-2
eISBN: 978-1-5107-3023-6

Printed in China

Contents

Foreword

I grew up on the Swedish island of Öland, where early on I discovered the pleasures of cooking and baking. In my family, everyone always lent a hand in the kitchen, and whoever was cooking or baking was excused from cleaning up afterward (which suited me just fine, to be quite honest). As a teenager, I became obsessed with baking, plowing through one baking book after another.

As you've probably figured out, we were never without something to nibble on with our coffee at our place. In fact, shared mealtimes and coffee breaks were especially important to me when I was growing up, because this was when everyone took some time to sit down and really talk to one another.

I held on to that philosophy when I started my own family. With a husband and four children, we consume a lot of baked goods. And I don't mind in the least—on the contrary, because I absolutely love to bake! As most of the readers of my blog, jennysmatblogg.nu, are surely aware of by now, it's baking with candy that really kicks my imagination into high gear. Discovering unfamiliar items in the candy aisle has a poetic quality, because it enables me to experiment in the kitchen with ingredients that could add a touch of perfection to the next cake, cookie, or frozen dessert.

It is my sincere hope that the delight I take in baking with candy will excite you too, and that you'll find inspiration and happiness in the kitchen as I do. *Baking with Candy* will show you how to playfully recreate your favorite recipes by simply tweaking them with some added chocolate or candy. With so many delicious ingredients out there, you're bound to succeed!

—Jenny Warsén

SMALL BITES & TREATS

Gooey Mini Cookies with Nutella and Candy

Double Spritz Cookies with Nutella

Toffee Brittle with Peanuts

Chewy Chocolate Bar Cookies with Candy

Chewy Toffee Bar Cookies with Candy

Chocolate Balls with Nutella Filling

Crispy Squares

Toffee Squares

Swedish Macaroons with Daim

Candy Cane Macaroons

Chocolate Macaroons with Caramel and Peanuts

Lemon and Licorice Macaroons

Nutella Pastries

Gooey Mini Cookies with Nutella and Candy

These miniature, gooey cakes are luscious, soft, and slightly chewy.
Why not mix things up by adding your favorite candy?

makes about 14 cookies

2 large egg whites
1 cup confectioners' sugar
Scant ¼ cup all-purpose flour
4 tbsp cocoa
3⅓ oz Nutella, at room temperature
14 Dumle Original Toffees,[i] 42 mini
    marshmallows, or ½ cup Smarties[ii]

Preheat the oven to 350°F. Beat the egg whites and confectioners' sugar in a bowl with an electric mixer until the meringue develops stiff peaks and you can turn the bowl upside down without the contents sliding out.

Sift the flour and cocoa over the meringue and fold them in with a small spatula. Finally, fold in the Nutella to make a shiny, smooth batter.

On two baking sheets lined with parchment paper, portion out dots of batter, leaving a wide space between them, and press your chosen candy on top of the balls. (The Dumle should be at the center of the dot of batter, while other types of candy can be sprinkled over it.) Bake the cookies on the middle rack of the oven for 7 to 10 minutes. Let them cool a little before removing from the baking sheet.

Double Spritz Cookies with Nutella

These are tender cookies with Nutella filling. Thinking of using dulce de leche instead?
That's not a bad idea! It will be just as delicious.

makes about 12 cookies

3½ oz butter, at room temperature
Scant ¼ cup confectioners' sugar
1½ tbsp vanilla sugar
½ cup all-purpose flour
3⅓ oz potato flour[iii]
3⅓ oz Nutella, at room temperature

Preheat the oven to 350°F. Mix together the butter, confectioners' sugar, and vanilla sugar in a bowl. Add in the all-purpose flour and potato flour, alternating between the two, until you get a sticky dough.

Transfer the dough to a piping bag fitted with a star tip, and measure out 4 to 5 strips of dough onto a baking sheet lined with parchment paper. Bake the strips on the middle rack of the oven for about 10 to 12 minutes—they should color, but just barely. Cut the strips of dough into equal-sized pieces as soon as you pull them out of the oven.

Let the cookies cool completely. Place a pat of Nutella on half the cookies and place the other cookies on top like a lid.

Toffee Brittle with Peanuts

This super simple brittle comes together in a flash when unexpected visitors—or invited guests, for that matter—show up.

makes 12 pieces of brittle

12 Dumle Original Toffees or a
    similar candy
1 oz milk chocolate bar
1 oz salted peanuts, coarsely chopped

Preheat the oven to 350°F. Space the Dumle toffees as far apart as possible on a baking sheet lined with parchment paper. Melt the chocolate over a water bath (bain-marie).

Bake the Dumle toffees for a few minutes. Keep a close eye on them—they'll be ready when they begin to pool and look like chips. Sprinkle the peanuts over them immediately, and then drizzle with the chocolate. Let the brittle cool, and serve. Store in the refrigerator.

Chewy Chocolate Bar Cookies with Candy

For this recipe, use Malaco Kick Bites Soft & Sweet Licorice Toffees,[iv] Dumle, or candy canes—if you have trouble making up your mind on which candies to use, go ahead and make all three! To make pretty candy cane cookies, save some of the crushed candy and sprinkle it on the baked cookies as soon as they come out of the oven.

makes about 40 cookies

7¾ oz butter, at room temperature
6¾ oz granulated sugar
5 tbsp Lyle's Golden Syrup[v]
2 cup + 2 tsp all-purpose flour
4 tbsp cocoa
1 tbsp vanilla sugar
1½ tsp baking powder
Approximately 5⅓ oz candy
    (for example, Malaco Kick Bites
    Soft & Sweet Licorice Toffees,
    Dumle Original Toffees, and/or
    candy canes)

Preheat the oven to 400°F. In a bowl, cream the butter and sugar, then add in the syrup. Mix the flour, cocoa, vanilla sugar, and baking powder together in another bowl, then stir the dry mixture into the butter mixture. Combine until it becomes a smooth dough.

Cut the soft candy into chunks and mix into the dough.

Candy canes: Insert one freezer bag into another, transfer the candy canes to the bags, and crush the candy with a mallet. Save some of the crushed pieces for garnish, and work the rest of the candy into the dough.

Break the dough up into 3 or 4 pieces (depending how large you want the bars to be) and roll them into long strips. Place the strips of dough on a baking sheet lined with parchment paper, and pat them down a little with your fingers.

Bake the strips of dough on the middle rack of the oven for 8 to 11 minutes, then cut them into diagonal bars while they're still warm.

For candy cane bars: sprinkle the saved crushed candy over the dough immediately after removing the baking sheet from the oven. Let the cookies cool completely on a cooling rack.

Chewy Toffee Bar Cookies with Candy

This is a fun little cookie bar that's easy to customize with your favorite candy. I've baked them with Dumle Original Toffees, Malaco Kick Bites Sweet Licorice Toffees, Daim, and Ako Cream Toffees.[vi]

makes about 40 cookies

7¾ oz butter, at room temperature
6¾ oz granulated sugar
4 tbsp Lyle's Golden Syrup
2 cup + 2 tsp all-purpose flour
1 tbsp vanilla sugar
1½ tsp baking powder
Approximately 5⅓ oz candy (Dumle
    Original Toffees, Malaco Kick
    Bites Sweet Licorice Toffees,
    Daim, Ako Cream Toffees, or
    a similar candy)

Preheat the oven to 400°F. In a bowl, cream the butter and sugar, then mix in the syrup. In another bowl, mix the flour, vanilla sugar, and baking powder together, then work this into the butter mixture. Mix to make a smooth dough. Cut or chop the candy into chunks, and work them into the dough.

Break the dough up into 3 or 4 pieces (depending on how large you want the bars to be) and roll them into long strips. Place the strips of dough on a baking sheet lined with parchment paper, and pat them down a little with your fingers.

Bake the strips of dough on the middle rack of the oven for 8 to 11 minutes, until they have developed a nice color. Cut the strips of dough into diagonal slices while they're still warm. Let the bars cool completely on a rack.

Chocolate Balls with Nutella Filling

Create these sumptuous chocolate balls using creamy Nutella as a filling—they're always a hit. If you prefer, go ahead and fill each chocolate ball with a piece of Center[vii] milk chocolate–covered toffee instead, or a dollop of dulce de leche.

makes about 25 chocolate balls

5 oz Nutella
1¾ oz milk chocolate
Scant 3½ cup old-fashioned
   rolled oats
7 oz butter, at room temperature
1¼ cup confectioners' sugar
Scant ¼ cup O'Boy (or a similar brand)
   instant hot chocolate powder
2½ tbsp cocoa
2 tbsp cold coffee
Pinch of salt
Grated coconut or pearl sugar[viii]

Cover a tray with parchment paper, and spoon out 25 small balls of Nutella. Put the tray in the freezer, and start making the chocolate ball mix.

Carefully melt the milk chocolate over a water bath (bain-marie). Pulverize the rolled oats into smaller pieces in a food processor or blender.

In a bowl, make a batter by beating together the butter and confectioners' sugar with an electric mixer. Stir in the O'Boy instant powder, cocoa, coffee, and salt. Add in the rolled oats pieces and milk chocolate, and combine until you get a lump-free, dough-like batter. Let the dough chill in the refrigerator for 1 hour.

Remove the dough from the refrigerator and the Nutella from the freezer. Make balls using the dough, leaving an indentation in each ball with your thumb. Place a pat of Nutella into each indentation, and cover it with some more of the chocolate dough. Roll the balls in coconut flakes or pearl sugar.

Serve at room temperature, but store them in the refrigerator.

Crispy Squares

I often pass around Rice Krispies Treats when we have guests.
If—contrary to expectation—you have any leftovers, they freeze very well.

makes about 25 squares

8 oz peanut butter
3⅓ oz granulated sugar
3⅓ fl oz Lyle's Golden Syrup
3½–3¾ cup Rice Krispies
¼–½ cup grated coconut
1 tsp vanilla sugar
7 oz milk chocolate bar
1¾ oz dark chocolate bar

In a saucepan, warm up the peanut butter, sugar, and syrup until you have a smooth mixture. (Note: Do not bring to a boil!)

In a bowl, mix the Rice Krispies, grated coconut, and vanilla sugar. Stir in the peanut butter/sugar mixture and mix thoroughly, then spread it in an approximately 8" x 12" baking pan lined with parchment paper.

Melt the milk chocolate over a water bath (bain-marie), then spread it over the Rice Krispies mixture. Melt the dark chocolate and drizzle it over the layer of milk chocolate. Drag a fork through the dark chocolate to make a decorative pattern.

Put the pan in the refrigerator to chill until the chocolate has set. Cut the pan of Rice Krispies into squares, and store them in the refrigerator until time to serve.

Toffee Squares

Using a rectangular pan for baking is quick and easy, not to mention perfect for making party treats. This delicious shortbread dough—layered with wonderfully soft, chewy toffee and topped with chocolate—reminds me of a Twix candy bar and is a personal favorite.

makes about 20 small squares

Bottom layer
Scant 1¾ cup all-purpose flour
Scant ¼ cup granulated sugar
4½ oz butter, at room temperature

Toffee filling
Scant 6¼ oz butter
6¾ oz granulated sugar
1¼ cup heavy whipping cream
Scant ¼ cup Lyle's Golden Syrup

Chocolate topping
7 oz milk chocolate

Preheat the oven to 350°F. In a bowl, mix all the ingredients for the bottom layer and work it until it becomes a dough. Press the dough evenly into the bottom of an approximately 8" x 12" baking pan lined with parchment paper. Bake the dough for approximately 20 minutes.

In a large, heavy saucepan, stir in all ingredients for the toffee filling. Let the mixture cook over medium heat until it reaches 244.4°F–248°F; this will take about 30 minutes. Stir occasionally.

Spread the toffee mixture evenly over the bottom layer, and then put the pan in the refrigerator while you melt the chocolate over a water bath (bain-marie). Spread the melted chocolate over the toffee layer, and make a pretty pattern on top by dragging a fork across the chocolate.

Let chill in the refrigerator until the chocolate has set a little, and then cut into squares with a sharp knife. Store the squares in the refrigerator. Bring them up to room temperature for about 20 minutes before serving.

Swedish Macaroons with Daim

*Swedish macaroons are on my top-three list of favorite pastries.
And they're so fun and easy to update with different flavors and toppings.
These macaroons just vanish off the plate at coffee breaks in our home.*

makes about 20 large or 30 small macaroons

Bottom layer
10½ oz almond paste
1 extra-large egg white
5 oz granulated sugar

Filling
8¾ oz butter, at room temperature
1½ cup confectioners' sugar
3 chopped Double Daim[ix] or a similar
   candy (6 oz total weight)
1 tsp vanilla sugar
1 extra-large egg yolk

Topping
10½ oz milk chocolate bar
Toffee crumbles or crushed Daim

Preheat the oven to 350°F. Grate the almond paste into a bowl, and mix it with the egg white and granulated sugar to make a thick batter. Pipe or spoon out the batter (to make the individual bottom layers) onto a baking sheet lined with parchment paper, and bake on the middle rack of the oven for 10 to 15 minutes. The layers should color slightly but retain some chewiness in the middle. Let the layers cool before loosening them from the paper.

In a bowl, whisk together all the ingredients for the filling to make a smooth cream. Spread a layer of this cream filling on the underside (the side facing the parchment paper) of each layer. Let the macaroons chill in the refrigerator or freezer for at least 1 hour.

Melt the chocolate in a water bath (bain-marie), and let it cool down slightly. Quickly dip the macaroons' cream side in the melted chocolate, letting the excess chocolate drip off, and place the macaroons on a sheet of parchment paper. Immediately sprinkle them with some toffee crumbles or crushed Daim. Keep the macaroons in the refrigerator until set. Bring them up to room temperature before serving. These macaroons can be frozen.

Candy Cane Macaroons

These macaroons get their fresh, minty flavor and lovely crunch from candy canes. Crushed candy cane is useful in a lot of sweets. Whenever you seek a fresh, mint flavor—think candy canes!

makes 20 large or 30 small macaroons

Bottom layer
10½ oz almond paste
1 extra-large egg white
5 oz granulated sugar

Filling
8¾ oz butter, at room temperature
1½ cup confectioners' sugar
1 tsp vanilla sugar
1 extra-large egg yolk
5–6 drops peppermint extract, or to taste
3⅓ oz candy cane, finely crushed

Topping
10½ oz dark chocolate bar, 55–70 percent cocoa
Approximately ¼ cup finely crushed candy cane

Preheat the oven to 350°F. Grate the almond paste into a bowl, and mix it with the egg white and granulated sugar to make a thick batter. Pipe or spoon out the batter (to make the individual bottom layers) onto a baking sheet lined with parchment paper, and bake on the middle rack of the oven for 10 to 15 minutes. The bottoms should have some color but the center should remain a bit chewy. Let the layers cool before loosening them from the paper.

In a bowl, whisk together all the ingredients for the filling to make a smooth cream. Spread a layer of this cream filling on the underside (the side facing the parchment paper) of each macaroon layer. Try to mound the filling in the center to make a top. Let the macaroons chill in the refrigerator or freezer for at least 1 hour.

Melt the chocolate in a water bath (bain-marie), and then let it cool down slightly. Quickly dip the macaroons' cream side in the melted chocolate and let the excess drip off. Put the macaroons on a sheet of parchment paper and immediately sprinkle them with some crushed candy cane. Put the macaroons in the refrigerator until set. Bring them up to room temperature before serving. These macaroons can be frozen.

Chocolate Macaroons with Caramel and Peanuts

These macaroons remind me of a Snickers bar and are dangerously tempting!

makes 20 large or 30 small macaroons

Bottom layer
10½ oz almond paste
1 extra-large egg white
5 oz granulated sugar

Filling 1
7 oz milk chocolate bar
8¾ oz butter, at room temperature
1¼ cup confectioners' sugar
1 extra-large egg yolk

Filling 2
½ container (7 oz) dulce de
  leche, chilled

Topping
10½ oz milk chocolate bar
Salted peanuts, coarsely chopped

Preheat the oven to 350°F. In a bowl, grate the almond paste and mix it with the egg white and granulated sugar to make a thick batter. Pipe or spoon the batter out (for the individual bottom layers) onto a baking sheet lined with parchment paper. Bake the layers on the middle rack of the oven for 10 to 15 minutes, until they have some color but the centers are still chewy. Let the layers cool before loosening them from the paper.

For Filling 1, melt the chocolate over a water bath (bain-marie). Let the chocolate cool, then mix it with the remaining ingredients to make a smooth cream.

For Filling 2, drop a teaspoonful of dulce de leche on the underside (the side facing the parchment paper) of each layer, and then spread on the cream filling (as best you can). Chill the macaroons in the refrigerator or freezer for at least 1 hour.

For the topping, melt the chocolate over a water bath and let it cool a little. Quickly dip the macaroons' cream side in the chocolate and let the excess drip off. Put the macaroons on a sheet of parchment paper. Immediately sprinkle them with the chopped peanuts and put the macaroons back in the refrigerator to set. Bring them up to room temperature before serving. These macaroons can be frozen.

Lemon and Licorice Macaroons

*Lemon and licorice is a wonderful flavor combination! If you haven't tried it yet,
I recommend it wholeheartedly. Why not start with this recipe?*

makes 20 big or 30 small macaroons

Bottom layer
10½ oz almond paste
1 extra-large egg white
5 oz granulated sugar

Filling
8¾ oz butter, at room temperature
1 extra-large egg yolk
1½ cup confectioners' sugar
Grated zest and juice from ½ lemon
1 tbsp vanilla sugar

Topping
10½ oz milk chocolate bar
Licorice sprinkles (crush hard
    licorice candies)

Preheat the oven to 350°F. In a bowl, grate the almond paste and mix it with the egg white and granulated sugar to make a thick batter. Pipe or spoon the batter out (for the individual bottom layers) onto a baking sheet lined with parchment paper. Bake the layers on the middle rack of the oven for 10 to 15 minutes, until they have some color but the centers are still chewy. Let the layers cool before loosening them from the paper.

In a bowl, whisk together all the ingredients for the filling. Taste the filling to ensure that it's as lemony as you like it. Spread a layer of cream filling on the layers' underside (the side facing the paper). Chill the macaroons in the refrigerator or freezer for at least 1 hour.

Melt the chocolate over a water bath (bain-marie) and let it cool down slightly. Quickly dip the macaroons' cream side in the chocolate and let the excess drip off, and then put the macaroons on a sheet of parchment paper. Immediately sprinkle them with some licorice sprinkles. Chill the macaroons in the refrigerator until set. Bring them up to room temperature before serving. These macaroons can be frozen.

Nutella Pastries

These crispy-layered pastries are a snap to make and will delight anyone who loves Nutella.
They're perfect for when coffee guests show up at your door out of the blue.

makes 4 pastries

4 sheets of frozen puff pastry
    (they need to be defrosted
    for about 15 minutes)
3⅓ oz–5 oz Nutella, at room
    temperature
1 large egg, beaten lightly
2 tbsp flaked almonds
Confectioners' sugar, for dusting

Preheat the oven to 425°F. Press out the puff pastry a little with your hands. Drop a few tablespoons of Nutella in the middle of each sheet. Fold the sheets into parcels, press down the edges, and seal them with a fork.

Transfer the parcels to a baking sheet lined with parchment paper and brush them with some beaten egg. Sprinkle them with flaked almonds and bake on the middle rack of the oven for about 10 minutes, or until the pastries are golden brown and crisp. Dust with Confectioners' sugar and serve immediately.

GOOEY CAKES & BROWNIES

Gooey Cake with Cloetta Center Pralines

Gooey Cake with Salmiak Licorice and Raspberries

Gooey Cake with Nutella

White Gooey Cake with Raspberry Whipped Cream

Gooey Cake with Daim

Rocky Road Gooey Cake

Brownies with Toffee Sauce and Caramelized Popcorn

Molten Chocolate Cakes

Mug Cakes with Chocolate Caramels

Gooey Cake with Cloetta Center Pralines

There are no limits to how we can customize gooey cakes. Try out different types of candy, such as Cloetta Center pralines, which are used in this recipe. You're guaranteed new coffee break favorites.

serves about 12

5⅓ oz butter
Breadcrumbs, for dusting
4 large eggs
Scant 1¾ cup granulated sugar
1 tsp vanilla sugar
6¾ oz all-purpose flour
4–5 tbsp cocoa
Pinch of salt flakes
1 roll (2¾ oz) Cloetta Center pralines
   (soft toffees covered in milk
   chocolate), or a similar candy

Chocolate frosting
7 oz milk chocolate bar
1¾ oz white chocolate bar (optional)

Preheat the oven to 350°F. Butter an approximately 8¾" to 9½" (22–24 cm) springform pan and dust it with finely crushed breadcrumbs.

Melt the butter, and let it cool down a little. In a separate bowl, mix the eggs and sugar. In another bowl, mix the flour, cocoa, and salt, and add them to the egg batter. Finally, add in the melted butter to make a smooth, lump-free batter. (Note: Do not whisk!)

Place the pralines over the bottom of the springform pan and pour the batter evenly over the candy. Bake on the middle rack of the oven for 20 to 25 minutes. (The cake should not be set in the center; it will firm up some once it has been transferred to the refrigerator.) Let the cake chill in the refrigerator for at least 4 hours.

To make the frosting, melt the chocolates in separate bowls. (You can omit the white chocolate, as it is only used for decoration.) Cover the cake with milk chocolate, and drizzle with white chocolate, if using.

Gooey Cake with Salmiak Licorice and Raspberries

Do you like salty Turkish Pepper[xi] and chocolate? If so, this cake is for you. The contrast from the raspberries' fresh, mild tang also imbues the cake with an extra dimension of flavor.

serves about 12

5¼ oz butter
Breadcrumbs, for dusting
10 pieces of Turkish Pepper
    salty licorice
4 large eggs
Scant 1¾ cup granulated sugar
1 tsp vanilla sugar
5 tbsp cocoa
6¾ oz all-purpose flour
Pinch of salt flakes
20 fresh raspberries + a few extra,
    for garnish
Confectioners' sugar, for dusting

Preheat the oven to 350°F. Butter a 8¾" to 9½" springform pan and dust it with finely crushed breadcrumbs.

Melt the butter, and let it cool down a little. Transfer the pieces of Turkish Pepper to double freezer bags, and crush them with a hammer.

In a bowl, mix the eggs and sugar. In another bowl, mix the cocoa, flour, and salt, and add them to the egg mixture. Finally, add in the melted butter and combine thoroughly. (Note: Do not whisk!)

Spread the raspberries at the bottom of the springform pan and pour the batter evenly over them. Bake on the middle rack of the oven for 20 to 25 minutes. (The cake will not be set in the center; it will firm up some once it has chilled in the refrigerator.) Chill the cake in the refrigerator for at least 4 hours. Garnish with raspberries and dust the cake with confectioners' sugar before serving.

Gooey Cake with Nutella

This is a creamy, Nutella-rich, all-around wonderful gooey cake. For a beautiful design, I placed a piece of lace cloth or a doily over the cake, dusted it with a generous amount of confectioners' sugar, and removed the lace carefully.

serves about 12

5¼ oz butter
Breadcrumbs, for dusting
4 large eggs
Scant 1¾ cup granulated sugar
1 tsp vanilla sugar
5 tbsp cocoa
6¾ oz all-purpose flour
Pinch of salt flakes
3⅓ oz Nutella, at room temperature
Confectioners' sugar, for dusting

Preheat the oven to 350°F. Butter an approximately 8¾" to 9½" springform pan and dust it with finely crushed breadcrumbs.

Melt the butter and let it cool a little. In a separate bowl, mix the eggs and sugar. In another bowl, mix the cocoa, flour, and salt, and then add them to the egg mixture. Finally, stir in the melted, cooled butter and the Nutella, and mix thoroughly to make a smooth batter. (Note: Do not whisk!).

Spread the batter evenly in the springform pan and bake on the middle rack of the oven for 20 to 25 minutes. (The cake will not be set in the center; it will firm up some once it has chilled in the refrigerator.) Let the cooled cake chill in the refrigerator for at least 4 hours. Dust with confectioners' sugar before serving.

White Gooey Cake with Raspberry Whipped Cream

*The flavors of white chocolate and raspberries pair up beautifully,
so this gooey cake usually disappears in a flash!*

serves about 12

7 oz butter
Breadcrumbs, for dusting
8¾ oz white chocolate bar
4 large eggs
1 cup granulated sugar
1 cup all-purpose flour
Confectioners' sugar, for dusting

Raspberry whipped cream
4½ oz fresh raspberries
1 cup heavy whipping cream
2 tbsp confectioners' sugar

Preheat the oven to 350°F. Butter a 9½" springform pan and dust it with finely crushed breadcrumbs.

In a saucepan, melt the butter and chocolate over low heat. Add in the eggs, sugar, and flour, and stir with a small spatula until you have a smooth batter. Spread the batter evenly in the springform pan.

Bake on the middle rack of the oven for 20 to 25 minutes. (The cake won't be set in the center, but will firm up some once it has chilled in the refrigerator.) Chill the cake in the refrigerator for at least 4 hours.

Mash the raspberries (perhaps save some for garnish) for the cream. Whip the cream into soft peaks, add the mashed raspberries and the confectioners' sugar, and mix it all together.

Dust confectioners' sugar over the cake and serve it with the raspberry whipped cream.

Gooey Cake with Daim

This is a classic dessert at our house.
We like to make it for dinner parties instead of a more elaborate cake.

serves about 12

5⅓ oz butter
Breadcrumbs, for dusting
4 large eggs
Scant 1¾ cup granulated sugar
1 tsp vanilla sugar
5 tbsp cocoa
6¾ oz all-purpose flour
Pinch of salt flakes

Frosting
1¼ cup heavy whipping cream
2 Double Daim or similar candy
   (4 oz total weight)

Preheat the oven to 350°F. Butter an approximately 8¾" to 9½" springform pan and dust it with finely crushed breadcrumbs.

Melt the butter and let it cool down a little. In a separate bowl, mix the eggs and sugar. In another bowl, mix the dry ingredients, then add them to the egg mixture. Finally, add in the melted butter to make a smooth, lump-free batter. (Note: Do not whisk!)

Spread the batter evenly in the springform pan. Bake on the middle rack of the oven for 20 to 25 minutes. (The cake won't be set in the center, but will firm up some once it has chilled in the refrigerator.) Chill the cake in the refrigerator for at least 4 hours.

Whip the cream into soft peaks, and coarsely chop the chocolate-covered toffee bars. Spread the cream over the cake and sprinkle with chocolate/toffee pieces.

Rocky Road Gooey Cake

This gooey cake has it all: salted peanuts, sweet caramel sauce, chewy Dumle toffees, and marshmallows.

makes about 12 pieces

5¼ oz butter
Breadcrumbs, for dusting
4 large eggs
Scant 1¾ cup granulated sugar
1 tsp vanilla sugar
5 tbsp cocoa
6¾ oz all-purpose flour
Pinch of salt flakes
½ container (7 oz) dulce de leche

Frosting
½ container (7 oz) dulce de leche
Splash of heavy whipping cream
Salted peanuts
Dumle toffees or a similar candy,
    cut in half
Mini marshmallows

Preheat the oven to 350°F. Butter an approximately 8¾" to 9½" springform pan and dust it with finely crushed breadcrumbs.

Melt the butter and let it cool down a little. In a separate bowl, mix the eggs and sugar. In another bowl, mix the cocoa, flour, and salt, then add them to the egg mixture. Finally, add in the melted butter to make a smooth, lump-free batter. (Note: Do not whisk!)

Spread the batter evenly in the springform pan. Bake on the middle rack of the oven for 20 to 25 minutes. (The cake won't be set in the center, but will firm up some once it has been chilled in the refrigerator.) Chill the cake in the refrigerator for at least 4 hours.

Stir the dulce de leche and a splash of (non-whipped) whipping cream together to make a caramel sauce. Drizzle the sauce over the cake and sprinkle with salted peanuts, Dumle toffees, and mini marshmallows.

Brownies with Caramel Sauce and Caramelized Popcorn

These delights are a cinch to make, especially if using store-bought caramelized popcorn and caramel sauce out of a jar.

makes 1 tray — 9 x 12

7 oz butter
Scant 1¾ cup granulated sugar
1¼ cup all-purpose flour
6¾ oz cocoa
2 tsp vanilla sugar
1 tsp baking powder
4 large eggs, at room temperature
2 pinches of salt flakes

Frosting
Caramel sauce (see p. 51
    for instructions)
Caramelized popcorn

Preheat the oven to 300°F. Line a 9" x 12" baking pan with parchment paper.

In a saucepan, melt the butter and sugar. In a bowl, mix together the dry ingredients, then whisk in the butter/sugar mixture. Add in the eggs and salt, and whisk to make a smooth batter.

Spread the batter evenly in the pan and bake the cake on the middle rack of the oven for about 18 to 20 minutes. It shouldn't be completely set in the center. Let it cool and then frost it with the caramel sauce and caramelized popcorn. Cut into squares.

Molten Chocolate Cakes

A true molten chocolate cake should have a firm, crisp surface but a soft, runny center.
They're even more lovely with some added caramel in the middle.

serves 4

2 large eggs
2 egg yolks
3 tbsp granulated sugar
3½ oz butter
3½ oz dark chocolate bar
3 tbsp all-purpose flour
4 Dumle toffees, 4 pieces of similar
    candy, or 4 tbsp dulce de leche
4 pinches of salt flakes

Garnish
Confectioners' sugar
Fresh berries
Sprigs of lemon balm (optional)

Preheat the oven to 425°F. In a bowl, beat the eggs, egg yolks, and sugar with an electric mixer until light and fluffy.

In a saucepan, melt the butter. Remove the saucepan from the heat; break the chocolate into the butter and let it melt, stirring constantly. Add the butter/chocolate mixture to the egg batter, sift in the flour, and combine until you have a smooth batter.

Butter four oven-proof ramekins, and fill them halfway with batter. Push one Dumle toffee or a tablespoon of dulce de leche into the batter at the center of each cake. Sprinkle with some salt flakes, and cover with the remaining batter.

Bake the cakes on the middle rack of the oven for 7 to 8 minutes. Remove the cakes from the oven and turn them carefully out onto plates. Cut a small slit into the edge of each cake to let some of the filling seep through. Dust with confectioners' sugar and garnish with berries and, if desired, a few sprigs of lemon balm. Serve immediately.

Mug Cakes with Chocolate Caramels

These soft and sticky chocolate cakes are cooked in the microwave, and take only 5 minutes to make. They're perfect for when time is short and the sugar monster rears its head!

serves 2

4 tbsp all-purpose flour
4 tbsp granulated sugar
3 tbsp cocoa
1 large egg
3 tbsp vegetable oil
3 tbsp milk
4 Riesen caramels, Dumle toffees, Cloetta Center pralines, or dollops of Nutella

For serving
Lightly whipped cream
Fresh berries
Store-bought chocolate nougat sauce (optional)
Sprigs of lemon balm, for garnish (optional)

In a bowl, mix all the ingredients except the candy, and stir until you have a lump-free batter. Fill the cups with batter to a little over ¾ full. Press some Riesen caramels or other melty candy into the batter.

In the microwave, heat one cup at a time for about 1 to 2 minutes on the highest setting. Microwaves do vary in power, so you may have to experiment a little. My mug cakes come out perfect after 1½ minutes.

Serve immediately with whipped cream, fresh berries, and some chocolate nougat sauce perhaps; and why not garnish your cake with a few sprigs of lemon balm?

PIES, TARTS, & CAKES

Daim Pie with Lemon Curd Whipped Cream

Caramel Tart with Licorice Sprinkles

Chocolate Ball Cake

Frozen Nutella Cake with Double Chocolate Nougat

Marshmallow Cake

Swedish Macaroon Cake with Daim

Chocolate Cake with Maltesers

Frozen Cheesecake with Chocolate, Caramel, and Peanuts

Mousse Cheesecake with Milk Chocolate and Cloetta Center Pralines

Daim Pie with Lemon Curd Whipped Cream

This pie has a tender bottom layer and a delicious caramel filling, and is topped with crunchy chocolate-covered pieces of toffee. It's sublime! And the whipped cream infused with lemon curd provides such a fresh and lovely contrast of flavors.

serves 10 to 12

Bottom layer
1¼ cup all-purpose flour
Scant 4½ oz butter, at room temperature
2 tbsp granulated sugar
1 large egg yolk

Filling
3½ oz butter
2 large eggs
5 oz brown sugar
3⅓ fl oz Lyle's Golden Syrup
1 tsp vanilla sugar
⅕ tsp salt
2 Double Daim (4 oz)

Lemon Curd Whipped Cream
2¼ cup heavy whipping cream
3⅓ fl oz lemon curd

Preheat the oven to 300°F.

In a bowl, mix all the ingredients for the bottom layer and work them into a dough. Press the dough into a pie pan measuring approximately 9½" to 10 ¼" in diameter. Prebake the bottom layer for 10 minutes.

In a saucepan, melt the butter for the filling and let it cool. In a bowl, combine the eggs, brown sugar, syrup, vanilla sugar, and salt. Add in the cooled butter. Pour the filling into the crust and bake the pie on the lower rack of the oven for about 40 minutes.

Chop the chocolate-covered toffee bars into small chunks and sprinkle them over the still-warm pie. Let the pie cool.

Whip the cream and mix in the lemon curd. Serve with the pie.

Caramel Tart with Licorice Sprinkles

This is a no-bake, no-oven required tart. Are you craving something special for your Sunday coffee break? Just remember that it needs to be refrigerated for 2 hours to allow it to set.

serves 10 to 12

Bottom layer
½ packet (about 7 oz) digestive
    biscuits
Approximately 2 oz melted butter
    (increase this amount for a less
    crumbly crust)

Filling
14 oz dulce de leche

Chocolate ganache
3⅓ fl oz heavy whipping cream
Approximately ¾ lb milk chocolate bar
2 pinches of salt flakes
Licorice sprinkles, for garnish

Crush the biscuits into small crumbs, either by hand or in a food processor. In a bowl, mix the crumbs and melted butter. Spread the mixture evenly in a pie pan measuring approximately 9½" in diameter. Chill in the refrigerator for 20 minutes.

Remove the pie pan from the refrigerator and spread the dulce de leche evenly over the bottom layer. Return the pan to the refrigerator.

In a saucepan, bring the cream to a boil, stirring occasionally. Remove the pan from the heat and break the chocolate into the warm cream. Stir the cream while the chocolate melts, and add in the salt flakes. Spread this chocolate ganache over the filling, and garnish with the licorice sprinkles.

Chill the tart in the refrigerator for about 2 hours before serving.

Chocolate Ball Cake

*Seriously, don't you feel a pang of a craving when you see this little treat?
There's something magical about these chocolate treats—they're always a hit with people of all
ages. And this cake is so pretty that you can't just look at it—you must have a taste!*

serves about 8

1¾ oz milk chocolate
Scant 3½ cup old-fashioned
    rolled oats
7 oz butter, at room temperature
1¼ cup confectioners' sugar
Pinch of salt
2 tbsp cold coffee
2½ tbsp cocoa
Scant ¼ cup O'Boy instant hot
    chocolate powder

Topping
Grated coconut
5 oz Nutella, at room temperature

Melt the chocolate carefully over a water bath (bain-marie). Crush the oats into smaller pieces in a food processor or blender.

In a bowl, whisk the butter and confectioners' sugar to make a smooth batter. Stir in the salt, coffee, cocoa, and O'Boy powder. Add the rolled oats and melted chocolate, and combine to make a smooth dough. Let the dough chill in the refrigerator for about 1 hour.

Use a little of the dough to roll mini chocolate balls; cover them in grated coconut and set them aside. Use the remaining dough to make a flat, round cake and transfer it to a platter. Cover the cake in grated coconut. Pile the mini chocolate balls into the middle of the cake. Pipe Nutella around the edge of the cake and serve.

Keep the cake in the refrigerator, and bring it up to room temperature 15 minutes before serving.

Frozen Nutella Cake with Double Chocolate Nougat

This is an absolutely delectable cake that's perfect for making a few days ahead when you have some time on your hands. All that's left to do before serving is take the cake out the freezer, add a little bit of garnish, and bask in the cries of delight when you set it on the table.

serves about 10

3½ oz slivered almonds
6½ oz lightly crushed meringues
2½ cup heavy whipping cream
14 oz can of sweetened
    condensed milk
13 oz jar of Nutella

Topping
1 double bar of double chocolate
    nougat (2¾ oz), frozen[xii]
Mini meringues

Toast the slivered almonds in a dry skillet until they're golden. Cover the bottom of a 9½" springform pan with crushed meringues. Transfer the rest of the crushed meringues to a bowl.

In another bowl, whip the cream until it begins to form soft peaks. Fold in the condensed milk, and mix until it's completely incorporated.

Warm the jar of Nutella carefully in the microwave, or place the jar in a warm water bath until its contents are lukewarm. Set aside about ¼ cup of Nutella; quickly fold the remainder of the jar and the whipped cream mixture (streaks are fine) into the crushed meringues. Layer the mixture and the toasted almonds in the springform pan.

Cover the pan with plastic wrap and put it in the freezer for at least 5 hours. Remove the cake 20 minutes before serving. Spread the reserved Nutella over the top, shave some chocolate nougat (you'll need to keep it in the freezer to do this) with a cheese slicer, and garnish the cake with nougat spirals and mini meringues.

Marshmallow Cake

A delicious, pastel-tinged cake—a star at any party!

serves about 12

Layers
3 large eggs
1¼ cup granulated sugar
Scant ¼ cup boiling water
1¼ cup all-purpose flour
1½ tsp baking powder
2½ tsp vanilla sugar

Raspberry filling
6¾ fl oz heavy whipping cream
8¾ oz Mascarpone cheese
5 oz fresh raspberries
3⅓ oz confectioners' sugar

Frosting
7 oz butter, at room temperature
Scant 1¾ cup confectioners' sugar
1 tbsp vanilla sugar

Garnish
Mini marshmallows in assorted colors

Preheat the oven to 350°F. Butter an approximately 7¾" x 8¾" springform pan and line the bottom with parchment paper.

In a bowl, beat the eggs and granulated sugar with an electric mixer until they're light and airy. Add in the water. In another bowl, mix the dry ingredients and fold them carefully into the egg mixture to make a smooth batter.

Pour the batter into the springform pan and bake for 30 to 35 minutes, or until the cake is done. Test it with a toothpick—if it comes out dry, the cake is ready. Let the cake cool in the pan, then loosen it carefully around the edge with a thin, sharp knife. Cover the cake with plastic wrap and put it in the freezer, preferably overnight, or until completely frozen.

Separate the partially or fully thawed cake into three layers; use a cake slice leveler if you have one.

In a bowl, whip the cream for the filling until it forms stiff peaks, then add in the mascarpone and mix thoroughly. In a shallow bowl, Mash the raspberries with the confectioners' sugar, then add this to the cream mixture and combine thoroughly. Sandwich the layers of cake with the cream mixture, and let the cake chill in the refrigerator overnight.

In a bowl, whisk together all the ingredients for the frosting. Cover the cake with frosting. (Set aside a bit of frosting; it can come in handy to glue on the marshmallows.) Garnish the cake with the marshmallows and serve.

Swedish Macaroon Cake with Daim

Swedish macaroons are among my favorite baked treats, so it was a lot of fun creating a cake featuring these goodies. It's very simple to make and almost absurdly delicious!

serves about 12

Bottom layer
¾ lb almond paste
2 large egg whites
Scant ¼ cup granulated sugar

Buttercream
3 Double Daim (6 oz total weight)
14 oz butter, at room temperature
2 large egg yolks
Scant 1¾ cup confectioners' sugar

Frosting
7 oz milk chocolate bar
1 Double Daim (2 oz total weight),
  coarsely chopped

Preheat the oven to 350°F. Line a 7¾" x 8¾" springform pan with parchment paper.

Grate the almond paste into a bowl. Add the egg whites and sugar, and mix to make a smooth batter. Spread the batter evenly in the pan and bake it on the middle rack of the oven for 20 to 25 minutes, or until the bottom is nicely browned. Put the pan in the refrigerator, and start making the buttercream.

In a bowl stir the butter, egg yolks, and confectioners' sugar to a smooth buttercream, and add the coarsely chopped Daim bars. Spread the buttercream over the macaroon layer and return it to the refrigerator.

Melt the milk chocolate over a water bath (bain-marie) and let it cool. Spread the chocolate over the buttercream. Sprinkle with chopped Daim. Chill the cake in the refrigerator and bring it up to room temperature 20 minutes before serving.

Chocolate Cake with Maltesers

Butter the springform pan but do not dust it with breadcrumbs; otherwise the crumbs will get into the frosting you're going to use for the cake. The layers of cake are easier to work with if they've been frozen, so I usually bake the layers a few days in advance and freeze them.

serves 10 to 12

Layers
5¼ oz butter
2 large eggs
1¼ cup granulated sugar
1 cup + 1 tsp all-purpose flour
2 tsp baking powder
Scant ¼ cup cocoa
1 tsp vanilla sugar
Pinch of salt flakes
5 fl oz boiling water

Lemon curd filling
Scant 1¾ cup heavy whipping cream
5 fl oz–6¾ fl oz lemon curd

Frosting
3½ oz butter, at room temperature
5¼ oz Philadelphia-style cream cheese
3⅓ oz Nutella, at room temperature
3⅓ oz dulce de leche
Scant 3⅓ oz confectioners' sugar
Scant ¼ cup cocoa
3⅓ fl oz heavy whipping cream

Garnish
Maltesers

Preheat the oven to 350°F. Butter a 7¾" springform pan and line the bottom with parchment paper.

In a saucepan, melt the butter for the cake layers, and whisk the eggs lightly in a cup. In a bowl, mix the dry ingredients, then stir in the eggs and the melted butter. Add the water and combine it to make a smooth batter. Pour the batter into the pan and bake it on the lower rack of the oven for 25 to 30 minutes, or until the cake is done. Test with a toothpick—if the toothpick comes out clean, the cake is ready.

Let the cake cool in the pan and loosen the sides carefully with a thin, sharp knife. Cover the cake with plastic wrap and put it in the freezer, preferably overnight, or until it is completely frozen.

Separate the partly or fully defrosted cake into three layers; a cake separator is a great help for this.

Whip the cream for the filling until it forms firm peaks, add in the lemon curd, and mix thoroughly. Sandwich the layers together with the cream/lemon curd mix in between. Chill the cake in the refrigerator overnight.

In a bowl, whisk all the ingredients (except the whipping cream) for the frosting, to make a fluffy cream. In another bowl, beat the whipping cream until soft peaks form, then combine it thoroughly with the other cream. Cover the cake with the frosting, garnish with Maltesers, and serve.

Frozen Cheesecake with Chocolate, Caramel, and Peanuts

I prefer making this cheesecake to an elaborate cream cake. There are three luscious ingredients: chocolate, salted peanuts, and caramel sauce—almost like a Snickers bar!

serves 12 to 14

Bottom layer
Scant 9 oz salted peanuts
½ container (7 oz) dulce de leche

Filling
3 large eggs
10½ oz Philadelphia-style
    cream cheese
Scant ½ cup granulated sugar
1 tbsp vanilla sugar
1¾ cup heavy whipping cream
7 oz milk chocolate, coarsely grated

Frosting
½ container (7 oz) dulce de leche
Approximately 3 tbsp heavy whipping
    cream
Salted peanuts

Set a scant ½ cup of peanuts aside for later. Coarsely chop the remaining peanuts. In a bowl, stir the chopped nuts into the dulce de leche. Flatten this mixture in the bottom of an approximately 9¾" springform pan, letting some of it go up the sides of the pan a bit.

Separate the egg yolks from the whites, and put them in separate bowls. Mix the egg yolks with the cream cheese, granulated sugar, and vanilla sugar to make a lump-free batter.

In another bowl, whip the cream with an electric mixer until peaks form. Use another—and completely clean—beater and bowl to whip the egg whites until stiff peaks form.

Carefully fold the yolk batter into the beaten egg whites, then mix in the whipped cream along with the grated chocolate. Spread the mixture over the bottom layer, cover the pan with plastic wrap, and put the cheesecake in the freezer for at least 5 hours, or preferably overnight.

Remove the cheesecake from the freezer 20 minutes before serving and loosen the edges. Stir together the dulce de leche and whipping cream to make a thick caramel sauce. Spread the caramel over the cake and sprinkle with the reserved peanuts.

Mousse Cheesecake with Milk Chocolate and Cloetta Center Pralines

No oven is required for this party-worthy cake. With its creamy chocolate mousse and Cloetta Center pralines, there's no doubt about it—this is one of my favorites.

serves about 12

Bottom layer
7 oz cookies (Maryland cookies, for example)
Scant 3 oz butter, melted

Mousse
3 sheets of gelatin or equivalent amount gelatin powder
14 oz milk chocolate
Approximately 1 lb Philadelphia-style cream cheese
½ lb Mascarpone cheese
1 cup heavy whipping cream
2 tbsp water
1 roll of Cloetta Center pralines

Garnish
Fresh raspberries
1 roll of Cloetta Center pralines

Crush the cookies into fine crumbs in a food processor or blender. Mix the butter and crumbs in a bowl and press the cookie crumb mixture into the bottom of an approximately 8¾" x 9½" springform pan.

Place the sheets of gelatin for the mousse to soak in cold water. (If using powdered gelatin, follow instructions on packet).

Melt the chocolate over a water bath (bain-marie). In a bowl, beat the mascarpone and cream cheese with an electric mixer. In another bowl, beat the whipping cream until it's stiff, then fold it into the cream cheese mixture, along with the chocolate. Mix thoroughly with a kitchen spatula.

Squeeze the water out of the sheets of gelatin and transfer them to a small saucepan with two tablespoons of water. Let the gelatin melt and add it in a stream into the cream cheese mixture in the bowl, stirring vigorously. Coarsely chop the pralines and fold them into the mousse.

Spread the mousse evenly over the bottom layer and chill the cake in the refrigerator for at least 5 hours, or preferably overnight.

Garnish the cheesecake with raspberries and coarsely chopped pralines right before serving.

ICE CREAM & PANNA COTTA

Fazer Tutti Frutti–Flavored Candy Ice Cream

Ice Cream with NonStop

Lemon Ice Cream with Sweet Licorice Ripple

Candy Cane Ice Cream

Panna Cotta with Kinder Egg Chocolate

Candy Panna Cotta with Sugary Gummy Peaches

Lemon Panna Cotta with Licorice Glaze

Mint Panna Cotta with Candy Cane Sprinkles

Striped Candy Panna Cotta

Tutti Frutti–Flavored Candy Ice Cream

This is candy ice cream of the first order! It's as popular with adults as with kids, and it's perfect for ice cream cones.

makes a scant 1 quart ~ 1 liter

1¾ cup heavy whipping cream

4¼ oz chewy Fazer Tutti Frutti candy[xiv]

14 oz can of sweetened condensed milk

Warm the cream and Tutti Frutti candy until the candy has melted, stirring continuously. Put the mixture in the refrigerator until it is completely chilled.

In a bowl, beat the chilled cream mixture with an electric mixer until it begins to form peaks. Fold in the sweetened condensed milk with a kitchen spatula until the mixture is smooth. Pour the mixture into a pan, cover it with plastic wrap, and put it in the freezer for at least 5 hours.

Ice Cream with NonStop

This is a festive and creamy candy ice cream that you can put together in just a few minutes. However, it must chill in the freezer for 5 hours before you can taste-test it.

makes about 1 quart ~ 1 liter

2¼ cup heavy whipping cream
14 oz can of sweetened
    condensed milk
Scant 9 oz NonStop[xiii]

In a bowl, whip the cream until it begins to form peaks. Add in the sweetened condensed milk, and fold it into the cream with a kitchen spatula until you have a smooth mixture. Add in the NonStop, setting a few aside for garnish.

Transfer the mixture to a pan and top with NonStop. Cover the pan with plastic wrap and put it in the freezer for at least 5 hours.

Lemon Ice Cream with Sweet Licorice Ripple

Lemon ice cream combined with licorice is at times the world's best treat—it's sweet, tangy, and a little bit salty. What true flavor sensations!

makes about 1 quart ~ 1 liter

Licorice ripple
6¾ fl oz heavy whipping cream
Scant ¼ cup granulated sugar
3⅓ fl oz Lyle's Golden Syrup
6 Malaco Kick Bites licorice
    toffees (4 oz)

Lemon ice cream
2¼ cup heavy whipping cream
Grated zest and juice from 2 lemons
14 oz can of sweetened
    condensed milk

Mix the cream, sugar, and syrup in a heavy saucepan. Chop the Kick Bites toffees into smaller chunks and stir them into the mixture in the saucepan. Cook on medium heat for about 25 minutes, or until the mixture has reached 250°F. Stir occasionally. Let the mixture cool in a cold-water bath.

In a bowl, whip the cream for the ice cream until stiff peaks form. (The lemons add extra liquid, so the cream must be firm). Add the lemon zest and juice along with the sweetened condensed milk, and fold them in with a spatula to make a smooth mixture.

Finish by drizzling the sweet licorice ripple into the ice cream mixture. Pour the mixture into a pan, cover it with plastic wrap, and put it in the freezer for at least 5 hours.

Candy Cane Ice Cream

Not only is this a great tasting ice cream, it's also a good treat to make when you need to blow off some steam. Joking aside, the best way to crush candy canes is to place them in double freezer bags and go at them with a hammer until nothing remains but fine candy cane sprinkles.

makes about 1 quart ⁓ 1 liter

2¼ cup heavy whipping cream
14 oz can sweetened condensed milk
A few drops of peppermint extract,
    or to taste
2 drops of red food coloring
10 small, crushed candy canes

Chocolate sauce
2¾ oz butter
1 cup confectioners' sugar
1 tsp vanilla sugar
2¾ oz dark chocolate bar (55–70
    percent cocoa)
6¾ fl oz heavy whipping cream

Whip the cream until it begins forming peaks. Add in the sweetened condensed milk along with the peppermint extract, and fold with a spatula to get a smooth mixture. Taste and add more peppermint extract if needed.

Divide the mixture between two bowls, and add the food coloring to one of the bowls. Layer the mixtures in a pan and top them with crushed candy canes.

Cover the pan with plastic wrap and put it in the freezer for at least 5 hours.

Melt the butter for the chocolate sauce in a small saucepan. Stir in the confectioners' sugar, vanilla sugar, and the chocolate, broken into pieces. Let it all melt together into a smooth mixture. Stir in the cream and bring everything to a boil. Take it off the heat. Ready!

Panna Cotta with Kinder Egg Chocolate

Childlike, yummy chocolate panna cotta! You can just as easily substitute the Kinder eggs for Kinder Riegel chocolate sticks. [xv]

serves 4 6

1½ sheets of gelatin (or equivalent amount in gelatin powder)
1 vanilla bean
1¼ cup heavy whipping cream
Scant ¼ cup granulated sugar
7 oz Philadelphia-style cream cheese
Approximately 3½ oz Kinder egg chocolate + some extra for garnish

Place the sheets of gelatin to soak in cold water. (If you're using gelatin powder, follow the instructions on the packet.)

Split the vanilla bean lengthwise and scrape out the seeds. Place the bean and the seeds in a saucepan together with the cream and sugar. Bring to a boil while stirring, then remove the pan from the heat. Remove the vanilla bean (rinse, dry, and save it for later use). Squeeze out the water from the sheets of gelatin and stir them thoroughly into the saucepan mixture (for powdered gelatin, follow the instructions on the packet). Add the cream cheese and stir until you have a lump-free mixture.

Melt the chocolate over a water bath (bain-marie), drizzle it into the saucepan mixture and fold it in a few times with a small ladle or a spatula. Pour the mixture into small decorative glasses and put them in the refrigerator for at least 4 hours. Top the glasses with bits of chocolate egg, or chocolate sticks.

Candy Panna Cotta with Sugary Gummy Peaches

This is a silky-smooth panna cotta that get its flavor from sweet and sour gummy candy peaches. Here I've chopped Tutti Frutti candy into small pieces for garnish, but any soft candy will do.

makes about 6 small servings

10 sugary gummy candy peaches
6¾ fl oz heavy whipping cream
4 tbsp granulated sugar

Garnish
Tutti Frutti candy

Place all the ingredients for the panna cotta in a saucepan. Bring to a boil while stirring, and make sure that all the candy peaches melt completely.

Pour the mixture into small decorative glasses, and put them in the refrigerator for at least 4 hours. Chop Tutti Frutti candy into small chunks and sprinkle them over the panna cotta before serving.

Lemon Panna Cotta with Licorice Glaze

A cool and attractive panna cotta that easily can be prepared the day before.

serves 4 to 6

2 sheets of gelatin (or equivalent
    amount in gelatin powder)
1¼ cup heavy whipping cream
7 oz Philadelphia-style cream cheese
1 vanilla bean
Scant ½ cup granulated sugar
Grated zest and juice from 1 lemon

Licorice glaze
1½–2 tbsp water
6 Malaco Kick Bites licorice toffees
    (4 oz total weight)

Soak the sheets of gelatin in cold water. (If you're using powdered gelatin, follow the instructions on the packet.)

Mix the cream and cream cheese in a saucepan. Split the vanilla bean lengthwise, scrape out the seeds, and put the seeds and the bean in the saucepan along with the sugar. Let the mixture simmer for a few minutes, stirring occasionally. Remove the saucepan from the heat, take out the vanilla bean (rinse, dry, and save it for later use). Squeeze out the water from the gelatin (for powdered gelatin, follow the instructions on the packet) and whisk it into the cream mixture. Add in the lemon zest and juice.

Pour the mixture into decorative glasses and put them in the refrigerator for at least 4 hours.

Pour the water for the licorice glaze into a small saucepan, break the Malaco Kick Bites into smaller pieces, and add them to the water. Let the toffees melt over low heat while stirring. Let the mixture cool, and then pour it over the panna cotta. Chill the panna cotta in the refrigerator for at least 1 hour before serving.

Mint Panna Cotta with Candy Cane Sprinkles

Panna cotta is the perfect dessert for those of you who like to prep things in advance so you can mingle with your guests. I typically make this the evening before a dinner party.

serves about 6

1½ sheets of gelatin (or equivalent in powdered gelatin)
1 vanilla bean
1¼ cup heavy whipping cream
Scant ¼ cup granulated sugar
7 oz Philadelphia-style cream cheese
A few drops of peppermint extract, or to taste

Garnish
12 small candy canes

Soak the sheets of gelatin in cold water. Split the vanilla bean lengthwise and scrape out the seeds. Place the bean and seeds in a saucepan along with the cream and the sugar.

Bring the mixture to a boil while stirring, and remove the vanilla bean (rinse, dry, and keep it for later use). Squeeze out the water from the sheets of gelatin (for powdered gelatin, follow the instructions on the packet) and add them to the saucepan. Mix in the gelatin thoroughly. Add in the cream cheese and stir until the mixture is smooth and without lumps. Add in the peppermint extract, drop by drop, until you're happy with the flavor.

Pour the mixture into decorative glasses, and put them in the refrigerator for at least 4 hours.

Transfer the candy canes to double freezer bags and crush them with a hammer. Sprinkle the crushed candy cane over the panna cotta before serving.

Striped Candy Panna Cotta

This candy-flavored panna cotta is sweet, creamy, and filling, and is best served in small glasses. If you'd like the colors to be more vivid, just add a drop of food coloring to the saucepan.

serves about 6

2 cups heavy whipping cream
1 bag Ahlgrens Bilar, marshmallow cars[xvi] candy

In a small saucepan, mix 5 fl oz of cream and 20 green candy cars, and warm the mixture over low heat until the candy has melted. Stir occasionally. Pour the mixture into small, decorative glasses, and put them in the refrigerator.

Start with the next layer: repeat the procedure but with 20 white cars this time. Let the mixture cool a little, then pour it on top of the first green layer.

Repeat the procedure, this time with the pink marshmallow cars. Chill the panna cotta in the refrigerator for at least 4 hours before serving.

CHRISTMAS CANDY

Marshmallow Santa Fudge

Chocolate Fudge with Crushed Candy Cane

Turkish Pepper Fudge

Caramel Fudge

Chocolate Bark with Crushed Candy Canes

Marshmallow Santa Fudge

*New flavors of marshmallow Santas are introduced every year.
Our family tradition is to include and enjoy them in at least one batch of fudge.*

makes approximately 30 pieces

12–14 marshmallow Santas
6¾ oz granulated sugar
2¾ oz butter
Scant ½ cup heavy whipping cream
5¾ oz white chocolate bar
Sprinkles

Line an approximately 6" x 6" pan with parchment paper. Chop the marshmallow Santas into small pieces.

In a saucepan, mix all the ingredients together except the white chocolate. Let everything melt over low heat, while stirring. Pull the saucepan from the heat, break the chocolate into pieces and add it to the mixture, while stirring. Stir until the chocolate has melted.

Pour the mixture into the parchment-lined pan, and sprinkle with sprinkles. Chill the pan in the refrigerator for a few hours, then cut the fudge into small squares. Store in the refrigerator.

Chocolate Fudge with Crushed Candy Canes

This is amazingly delicious fudge where the candy canes provide a fresh, minty flavor.

makes about 50 pieces

1¼ cup heavy whipping cream
1¼ cup granulated sugar
3⅓ fl oz Lyle's Golden Syrup
7 oz dark chocolate bar,
    55–70 percent cocoa
2¾ oz butter
½ cup crushed candy cane,
    for sprinkling (see the intro to the
    recipe, on p. 87)

Line an approximately 6" x 6" pan with parchment paper. In a heavy saucepan, mix the cream, sugar, and syrup, and heat the mixture to 250°F.

Remove the saucepan from the heat. Break the chocolate into pieces and add them to the mixture along with the butter. Stir until everything has melted, and the mixture is smooth and has a nice sheen.

Pour the mixture into the parchment paper–lined pan and sprinkle with the crushed candy canes. Chill the pan in the refrigerator for several hours before cutting the fudge into pieces. Store the fudge in the refrigerator.

Chocolate Fudge with Turkish Pepper

This is a creamy chocolate fudge with a hint of Turkish Pepper. The best of both worlds!

makes about 50 pieces

5¼ oz Turkish Pepper salmiak
  licorice candy
1¼ cup heavy whipping cream
Scant 1¾ cup granulated sugar
2¾ oz butter
4 tbsp Lyle's Golden Syrup
7 oz milk chocolate bar
Black food coloring

Line an approximately 6" x 8" pan with parchment paper. Crush the candies with a mortar and pestle, and save some for garnish.

Put all ingredients, except the chocolate, food coloring, and garnish, in a heavy saucepan. Heat the mixture up to 250°F while stirring.

Remove the saucepan from the heat. Break the chocolate into smaller pieces and add it to the mixture. Stir until the chocolate has melted.

Add the food coloring to the mixture, then pour it into the parchment-lined pan. Sprinkle with the crushed licorice candy and put the pan in the refrigerator for a few hours. Cut the fudge into even pieces and store it in the refrigerator.

Caramel Fudge

It's so much fun to create new versions of past, traditional Christmas candy recipes! This sweet, chewy fudge is guaranteed to become a new favorite on your Christmas candy table.

makes about 50 pieces

1¼ cup heavy whipping cream
1¼ cup granulated sugar
½ cup Lyle's Golden Syrup
2¾ oz butter
20 Dumle candies + 8 Dumle candies for garnish

Line an approximately 6" x 6" pan with parchment paper. Mix the cream, sugar, and syrup in a heavy saucepan and heat the mixture up to 250°F, while stirring.

Remove the saucepan from the heat, add the butter and 20 Dumle candies, and stir until the mixture is smooth and shiny.

Pour the mixture into the parchment paper-lined pan, top with coarsely chopped Dumle, and chill the fudge in the refrigerator for a few hours.

Cut the fudge into even pieces and store in the refrigerator.

Chocolate Bark with Crushed Candy Canes

*Candy making doesn't get any simpler than this!
It makes a both delicious and beautiful treat to offer anyone.*

makes about half a cookie sheet

3½ oz dark chocolate bar
    (55–70 percent cocoa)
3½ oz white chocolate
¼ cup crushed candy canes (see the
    intro to the recipe on p. 87)

Melt the dark chocolate over a water bath (bain-marie). Spread the melted chocolate in a thin layer over a cookie sheet lined with parchment paper and let it set.

Repeat this procedure with the white chocolate, spreading it in a thin layer on top of the dark chocolate. Immediately sprinkle crushed candy cane over the chocolates. Let it set completely. Break the bark into pieces and serve.

Recipe Index

ADDITIONAL NOTES REGARDING INGREDIENTS

i   See Amazon.com.

ii   Can be replaced with M&Ms.

iii Use potato flour—not potato starch. See Amazon.com and Bob's Red Mill. Potato flour is made from whole potatoes and used for baking. Potato starch is pure starch that is used as a thickening agent.

iv   See Amazon.com.

v   Some recipes use Swedish baking syrup, which is different from American syrup. Swedish syrup can be found at Amazon.com, or can be replaced with Lyle's Golden Syrup. I have put Lyle's in the recipes, as it is easily obtainable from well-stocked grocery stores.

vi   Can be replaced with Werther's Original Classic Cream Toffees.

vii Cloetta Center Original (78 gr/2¾ oz) Milk Chocolate Pralines with Soft Toffee Centers. See Amazon.com.

viii See Amazon.com.

ix   Can be replaced with Hershey's Skor.

x   Salty licorice candy with a very pronounced ammonia smell.

xi   Finnish salty salmiak licorice. See Amazon.com.

xii The recipe refers to double chocolate nougat. There are two kinds of nougat in Sweden: a smooth nougat made from hazelnuts sold in bar form, and a smooth, double chocolate nougat which is also sold in bar form. The author used the double chocolate nougat. Both nougats can be found at Amazon.com.

xiii Similar to M&Ms, except they are all dark chocolate.

xiv See Amazon.com.

xv   See Amazon.com.

xvi See Amazon.com.